POCKET GURUS
Guidance on the Go

Maureen Kelly

Portions of all Pocket Gurus proceeds will be donated to animal welfare organizations.

POCKET GURUS

Guidance on the Go

Maureen Kelly

© 2012 Maureen Kelly

First Edition

All rights reserved. No part of this book may be reproduced or transmitted in any form or by any means, electronic or mechanical, including photocopying, recording, or any information storage and retrieval system, without permission in writing from the Copyright owner. Address all inquiries to: sagebutterfly2@comcast.net (a division of sage butterfly design.)

ISBN-978-1-4675-3894-7

Dedication

To Francesco,
(St. Francis of Assisi)
a true Guru in the art
of loving and honoring all sentient beings.

(AND to all sentient beings).

TABLE OF CONTENTS

Introduction	vii
LOVE	2 - 3
ABUNDANCE	4 - 5
ADVENTURE	6 - 7
BALANCE	8 - 9
JOY	10 - 11
CHOICE	12 - 13
CLARITY	14 - 15
COURAGE	16 - 17
SURRENDER	18 - 19
DETACHMENT	20 - 21
TRUTH	22 - 23
POWER	24 - 25
SHINE	26 - 27
COMMUNICATION	28 - 29
INNOCENCE	30 - 31
TRUST	32 - 33
DANCE	34 - 35
COMPASSION	36 - 37
SILENCE	38 - 39
DREAM	40 - 41
STABILITY	42 - 43
PASSION	44 - 45
CELEBRATE	46 - 47
FLOW	48 - 49
GRATITUDE	50 - 51
PATIENCE	52 - 53
SING	54 - 55
BREATHE	56 - 57
MOTHER EARTH	58 - 59
SIMPLICITY	60 - 61
REST	62 - 63
PEACE	64 - 65
FORGIVENESS	66 - 67

continued...

TABLE OF CONTENTS

```
ECHO ............................................................... 68 - 69
CONNECTION .................................................. 70 - 71
TODAY .............................................................. 72 - 73
MAGIC .............................................................. 74 - 75
CELESTIAL BLESSINGS ..................................... 76 - 77
ABOUT THE AUTHOR ....................................... 79
```

INTRODUCTION

GURU - The syllable gu means shadows
The syllable ru, he who disperses them,
Because of the power to disperse darkness
the guru is thus named.
- *Advayataraka Upanishad 14—18, verse 5*

Welcome to the world of Pocket Gurus - Guidance on the Go, snippets of inspiration for busy lives and busy minds.

Some Gurus offer simple yoga poses, some are nature scenes, and some just emerged of their own free will from out of my pen. Along with each graphic comes an affirmation that may also assist in deepening that moment of 'time out.'

Sometimes in the midst of the everyday to-do lists and general life cacophony even a moment's pause - a brief respite from the chaos to regroup and breathe - can make all the difference.

It is my hope that these mini- Gurus will offer you that. This book can be used as an oracle, opening for random guidance, or just read through page by page to see which message resonates.

Blessings to you on your beautiful path. And it's also good to remember, as wise as these little guys are, the TRUE Guru lies within.

Namasté,
Maureen

Let's meet the Gurus.

> Love surrounds me
> and flows easily
> to and from my heart.

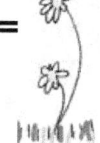

LOVE.

> The pot of gold
> is HERE.
> (Now.)

ABUNDANCE.

> No matter the direction
> I choose,
> life is a joyride.
> (If I allow it.)

ADVENTURE.

I celebrate balance
in body, mind, heart
and soul.

BALANCE.

Open and joyful,
I reach for the stars.

JOY.

> What I choose
> to 'see'
> becomes my reality.

CHOICE.

The clarity
I seek
is seeking
me.

CLARITY.

> Angels on
> either side of me,
> I know
> I cannot fall.

COURAGE.

> I surrender
> to the guidance
> of a
> Higher Power.

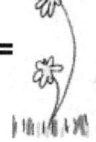

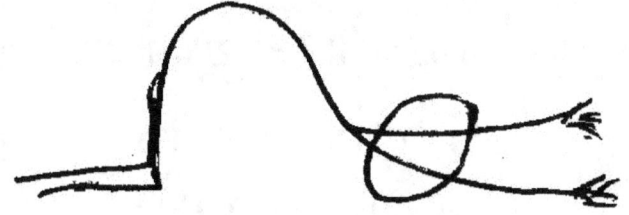

SURRENDER.

> I release what is
> no longer in alignment
> with the Spirit
> of who I AM.

DETACHMENT.

I speak my truth
from the
authenticity
of my heart.

TRUTH.

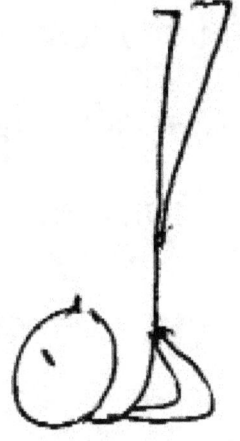

> I honor
> the Warrior Spirit
> within me.

I carry the sun
within me
and share the light.

SHINE.

When I listen
with the intent
to understand you
rather than the intent
to make you
see things my way,
then we are communicating.

COMMUNICATION.

Seeing everything as if
for the very first
(or last) time,
I realize that
only LOVE is real.

INNOCENCE.

I walk
the journey
with ease
and trust.

> I move
> to the groove
> of the Divine
> within me.

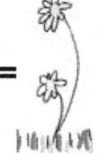

DANCE!

I honor
all sentient beings.

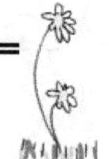

COMPASSION.

From within
the silence,
my soul speaks.

SILENCE....

> My dreams are
> being made
> manifest,
> as I honor my heart.

> Stable and secure,
> my roots are
> lovingly supported
> by Mother Earth.

STABILITY.

I open the door
of my heart
that my
passion might
walk through.

PASSION.

I celebrate
life
and the freedom
to be me.

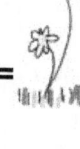

CELEBRATE!

No matter the size
of the waves,
I ride the tide
believing.

FLOW.

Grateful
for every breath
and every heartbeat,
I open myself
to the abundance of life.

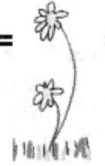

GRATITUDE.

Despite outward
appearances,
I know the sun waits
behind the clouds.

PATIENCE.

I joyfully share
the unique song
that lives in my heart.

I gratefully allow
the precious breath of life
to fill and inspire me!

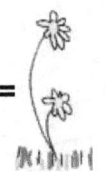

BREATHE.

> I affirm my love
> and devotion
> to our beautiful planet.

MOTHER EARTH.

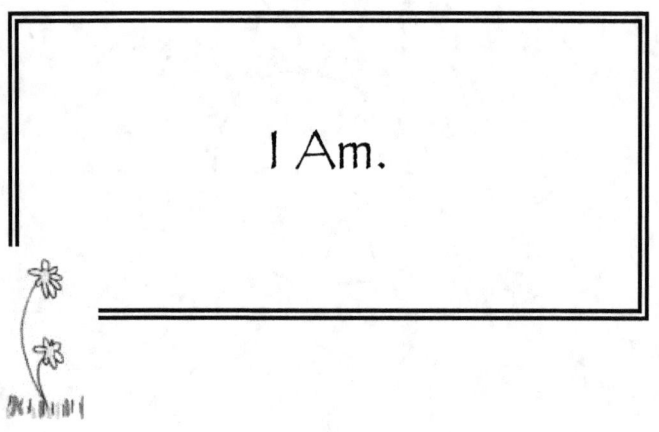

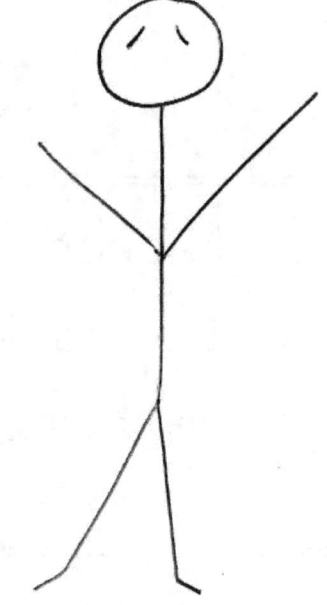

SIMPLICITY.

> I honor
> the ebb and flow
> of my being.

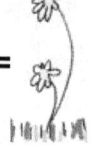

REST.

> As I breathe deeply
> into serenity
> and peace within,
> my outer world
> transforms.

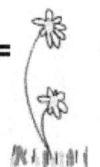

PEACE.

> As I forgive myself
> and all others
> in my life,
> I am free.

FORGIVENESS.

Everything
I do and say
comes back to me.

ECHO.

> I respect
> my connection
> with all of
> my sisters and brothers
> on the path.

CONNECTION.

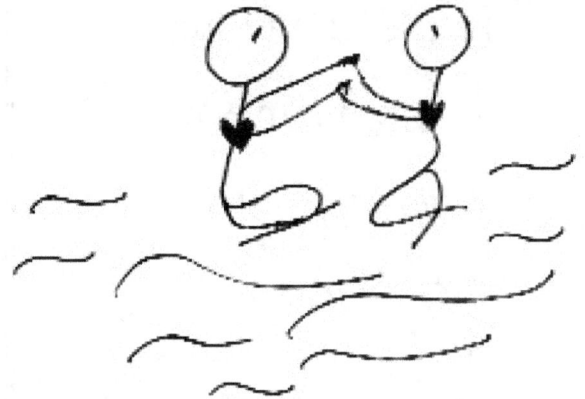

I celebrate life
from moment,
to moment
to moment...

TODAY.

I trust
in the
magic.

MAGIC.

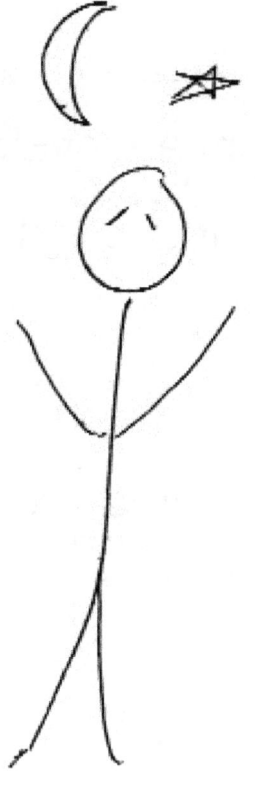

I am a traveler,
light and carefree...
on this
exquisite journey
called life.

CELESTIAL BLESSINGS.

Other books by Maureen:

WINE TYPES - DISCOVER YOUR INNER GRAPE
(www.winetypes.net)

PET TYPES - COMMUNING HEART TO HEART
(www.pet-types.net)

ENERGY TYPES -
PERSONALITY, CHAKRAS & BALANCE
(www.energy-types.net)

CHAKRA PLAY -
THE MAGICAL VIBRATION OF YOU
(www.energy-types.net)

For more info on POCKET GURUS please visit:
www.PocketGurus.net

To contact Maureen:
sagebutterfly2@comcast.net

ABOUT THE AUTHOR:

Originally from the San Francisco area, Maureen has lived in a variety of geographical locations including many years in Europe, several in both Washington, D.C. and Nashville, and currently, the Pacific Northwest. What she has learned from her sojourns in each of these places is that our real home is found within the heart.

A chakra yoga & meditation teacher and great advocate of sound healing, one of her greatest joys is learning new ways to promote balance and healing and sharing that with her yoginis and clients.

She cohabitates with five cats and two dogs and probably learns more from them than any other resource.

Life is an ongoing spiral of adventure and she is quite sure she will be introduced to many other Pocket Gurus on the path.

www.ingramcontent.com/pod-product-compliance
Lightning Source LLC
LaVergne TN
LVHW011736060526
838200LV00051B/3182